WORLD RELIGIONS

JUDAISM

Angela Wood

Wayland

For Hershel

who is more a -ness
than an -ism

First published in 1995 by
Wayland (Publishers) Ltd,
61 Western Road, Hove,
East Sussex BN3 1JD

This book was prepared for Wayland (Publishers) Ltd
by Ruth Nason

Book design: Alex Latham, Ken Alston

Typeset: A.J. Latham Limited,
Houghton Regis, Dunstable, Bedfordshire

Printed and bound in Italy by G. Canale & C.S.p.A., Turin

British Library Cataloguing in Publication Data
Wood, Angela
   Judaism. – (World Religions Series)
   I. Title II. Series
   296

ISBN 0-7502-1441-4

Acknowledgements

The author thanks the following for contributing to the book, by
talking about their life as a Jew, having their photograph taken,
making helpful suggestions and, above all, by their encouragement
and excitement: Jeremy Angel, the Berak family, the Bower
Ish-Horowicz family, Libby Burkeman, Yosef Chernobilsky, John
Curtis, Samuel Gilmore, Ester Gluck, Marcus Graichen, David
Gryn, Rabbi Hugo Gryn, Mehri Niknam, Lenny Nead, the
Oppenheimer family, Philip Ratner, Solomon Sananes, the
Silverman family, Maxwell Simon, Rabbi Jacqueline Tabick, Desi
Tammam, the children of Welwyn Garden City Synagogue.

The author and publishers thank the following for their permission
to reproduce photographs: Gordon Charatan: p. 34; Circa (Barrie
Searle: p. 41 (bottom); Anne Frank Stiftung: p. 12; Guy Hall:
pp. 1, 3, 6 (bottom), 28, 32, 41 (top), 45 (top); Robert Harding
Picture Library: pp. 7 (ASAP/Aliza Auerbach), 23 (ASAP/Joel
Fishman), 33 (PHOTRI), 35 (ASAP/J. Kaszemacher), 38
(ASAP/Israel Talby), 44 (PHOTRI); Hutchison Library (Liba
Taylor): pp. 6 (top), 30; Christine Osborne: pp. 5, 10, 13, 22, 24,
36 (bottom); TRIP: pp. 19 (M.O'Brien-Thumm), 21 (A. and B.
Peerless), 29 (R. Cracknell), 36 (top)(H. Rogers), 37 (H. Rogers);
Welwyn Garden City Hebrew Congregation: p. 45 (bottom);
Women's International Zionist Organization: pp. 15, 18. The pho-
tos on pp. 4, 8, 9, 15 (top), 20, 25, 26, 31, 39 and 40 were taken
by Angela Wood. The map on pp. 16-17 is drawn from a map by
Martin Gilbert.

Cover photo: Shabbat
candles (Barrie Searle,
Circa Photo Library).
Page 1: A Jewish mother
draws in the light of the
Shabbat candles.
Page 3: A rabbi shows two
young people the Torah
scroll. 'Turn it and turn it
for everything is in it.'

Contents

Around the world, Jews use Hebrew for prayers and Jewish study. In Israel, Hebrew is also the main everyday language of Jewish people. Jewish children there also learn Arabic and English at school.

INTRODUCTION

Who is a Jew?

There is a simple answer to this question. A Jew is someone who has a Jewish mother or who chooses to become Jewish. There are more complicated answers as well.

Being Jewish is *religious*: believing in one God, praying to God, keeping 'Shabbat' (the Sabbath) as a special day...

Being Jewish is *cultural*: enjoying Jewish songs, eating special foods, using certain expressions...

Being Jewish is *historical*: belonging to a people that is 4,000 years old and understanding that events in the past affect life today...

Being Jewish is *social*: being with other Jews and doing things together that help Jews to be themselves...

Being Jewish is *political*: being part of a people all over the world, with a spiritual home-land in Israel, and feeling that whatever happens to any Jew somehow happens to all Jews...

Absorbed in prayer at the Western Wall in the Old City of Jerusalem. This is the nearest spot to the site of the ancient Jewish temple. Many Jews go to pray there, in groups or on their own.

Orthodox, Reform, Conservative . . .

Many Jews are 'observant', that is, they lead a religious life. They practise their religion and culture in different ways, and there are various groups to which they might belong. Members of one family may belong to different groups, and some Jews relate to one group in one way and another group in another way. For example, some Jews are members of Orthodox synagogues but are not fully observant in their private lives, and some are members of Progressive synagogues but may be quite observant in their private lives.

These Hasidic Jews are choosing myrtle for the festival of Sukkot. The man on the right has a soft bag in which he carries his 'tallit' (prayer shawl).

Orthodox Jews believe that the 'Torah' (teaching) was given by God and can never change. They follow all the laws of their religion exactly. They always pray in Hebrew. Men and women have distinct and definite roles and responsibilities.

Reform Jews believe that the Torah has to be seen in a new way in every age. Some Jewish laws were made by people, and not by God, and so they can be changed. Reform Jews today keep more traditions than they used to. In Europe, there are also Liberal Jews, whose ideas are very similar to Reform. Sometimes Reform and Liberal Jews are called 'Progressive'.

ZIONISTS

Most Jews are Zionists. They support the State of Israel and its right to exist. They see Israel as a place of refuge and also as a place of inspiration. They give money for immigrants in Israel or for environmental projects, such as tree-planting.

Some but not all Zionists live in Israel. Outside Israel, people sometimes ask Zionists to explain something the Israeli government has done. Sometimes they even complain to the Zionists about it or hold them responsible.

The 'shofar' (ram's horn) is blown on Rosh Hashanah (the New Year).

Conservative Jews accept the idea that the Torah is given by God, but also believe that the religion must change if it is to be fully alive. They say that Jewish life can draw from other cultures and yet remain distinctly Jewish. Conservative Jews are found mostly in the USA but also in other countries, such as Israel and Britain, where they are called 'Masorti' (traditional).

There are also Jews today who are pleased to be Jewish and join in many celebrations, but who do not practise their religion completely – or at all. They are called 'secular' or 'cultural' Jews. Some do not believe in God. Some believe in God but find the Jewish religion too difficult to observe, or think that it has not changed enough in the modern world.

The Jewish people

There is no Hebrew word for 'Judaism' or even for 'religion'. The Hebrew word for the Jewish way of life, following Jewish law, is 'halaha', which means 'walking'.

At the festival of Purim many Jews wear fancy dress. When the story of Ester is read, they wave rattles or boo and hiss to drown Haman, the tyrant's name.

Sometimes people talk about the 'Jewish race', but there is really no such thing. Nor is there a 'Jewish nation'. It is better to speak about the 'Jewish people'. There are Jews of every race and nationality. You will meet some of them in this book.

1

THE STORY OF THE JEWS

The Jewish people have a long history, and their religion and culture have changed gradually over thousands of years. There have been several turning-points. Each of them tells us something about how Jews see the world and their place in it.

Abraham 'our father'

Abraham lived in the Middle East, about 4,000 years ago. People then believed in different gods for every part of life. They made idols and prayed to them. Abraham saw life as a whole, with everyone and every-thing connected, and he believed that there was just one God.

Abraham heard God telling him to take his family to a new place and start a new life, with new ideas. His people became the Hebrews, and the language they spoke, Hebrew, is still the main Jewish reli-gious language. The word means 'crossing over' and every Jew 'crosses over' in some way. When a person becomes Jewish, she or he takes a Hebrew name, such as Rachel or Noah, and is called '(Hebrew name), daughter/son of Abraham our father'.

The children of Israel

Abraham and Sarah had twin grandsons, Esau and Jacob. Jacob was jealous of Esau, who would inherit the authority of the family because he was the older of the two. Jacob deceived their father and tricked Esau out of his birthright, then ran away, scared.

An Arab and a Jew greet one another in Jerusalem.

JEWS AND MUSLIMS

Abraham had a son, Isaac, by his Hebrew wife, Sarah, and a son, Ishmael, by his Egyptian wife, Hagar. This means that both Jews and Muslims trace their ancestry to Abraham. Jews today who care about peace between Arabs and Israelis – and between Muslims and Jews – think of Arabs and Muslims as their spiritual cousins.

Years later, he plucked up courage to face Esau again. The night before they met, Jacob wrestled with a mysterious being in his sleep. He heard God say that he would be known from then as 'Israel', meaning someone who had struggled with God and survived. Jacob's descendants are called 'the children of Israel' and many Jews feel that it is a good name for them. Sometimes they struggle against God, questioning and wondering. Sometimes they struggle for God, trying to make the world better.

Israel is also the name for the land where the people settled. Today it is the only Jewish state in the world and is a homeland for many Jews.

Ben Yehuda Street in the New City of Jerusalem. Lubavitch Jews campaign to get Jews to observe their religion more fully. Here a young Jew has been persuaded to put on 't'filin' (small leather boxes containing Torah passages) and say his morning prayers. Ben Yehuda Street is named after Eliezer ben Yehuda, the 'father of modern Hebrew'. He founded the Hebrew Language Council in 1888.

Moses 'our teacher'

About 3,200 years ago, the children of Israel were slaves in Egypt and saw no escape. Then a series of miraculous events took place and they were freed. Moses led them towards the promised land, Israel. On the way, God gave Moses the Torah – the teaching by which the Jewish people live.

Jerusalem: exile and return

In about 1000 CE the people made Jerusalem on Mount Zion their capital and built a beautiful temple, where priests offered sacrifices to God. Four hundred years later, the Babylonians conquered them, destroyed the temple and took some people away. In Babylon, the people missed their temple and worshipped locally. They wrote a song about their sadness:

'By the rivers of Babylon, there we sat and wept as we thought of Zion... How can we sing a song of the Lord in a strange land? If I forget you, O Jerusalem, let my right hand wither; let my tongue stick to my palate if I cease to think of you, if I do not keep Jerusalem in memory even at my happiest hour.' *(Psalm 137: 1 – 5)*

Prophets are people who communicate with God in a special way. The prophet Jeremiah stayed in Jerusalem, but sent a letter, in the name of God, to the exiles in Babylon. He told them to get on with living and never to lose hope. They took his advice. After seventy years, they were allowed to return to Jerusalem, but most of them stayed. Since then, there have always been more Jews living outside Israel than inside.

A new temple was built in Jerusalem and, for a few hundred years, there were two main kinds of worship: sacrifices in the temple, and meetings, study and prayer in synagogues. Then, about 2,000 years ago, the Romans destroyed the temple when they occupied Israel.

In the New City of Jerusalem there is a model of the ancient walled city, as it was before the second temple was destroyed, in 70 CE.

JEREMIAH'S ADVICE

'Build houses and live in them, plant gardens and eat their fruit...
Multiply there and do not decrease. Seek the welfare of the city to which I have exiled you and pray to God on its behalf for in its prosperity you shall prosper.'
(Jeremiah 29: 5 – 7)

TIMELINE OF THE JEWISH PEOPLE

BCE

2000   Abraham's journey from Ur to Canaan.

1200   Escape from slavery in Egypt; giving of the Torah; entry into Israel.

1000   King David makes Jerusalem the capital of Israel.

900   King Solomon builds the temple in Jerusalem. The Jewish community in Ethiopia may date from this time.

586   Babylonians destroy the temple and deport Jews.

? 200   Jews settle in India.

168   Syrian Greeks occupy Israel, take over the temple for idol worship and try to make Jews abandon their religion. The Maccabees, Jewish freedom fighters, defeat them.

The festival of Hanukah recalls the restoration of temple worship in 168 BCE. Candles are lit in windows. The meaning is that all must be free to worship God.

Torah and Talmud

After the arrival of the Romans, Jews were dispersed through the Middle East and Europe, and created synagogues wherever they settled.

Study of the Torah became increasingly important, and wise or learned people who could teach about it were called 'rabbi' (my teacher). Most rabbis also had everyday jobs, so as to earn their livelihood. By the first century CE, adults met to discuss the Torah. Their discussions were remembered and written down, and later generations discussed these written accounts. The collection of discussions and decisions is called the 'Talmud'.

CE

70   Romans destroy the second temple and Jews are dispersed.

200   Yehudah HaNasi compiles and edits the first part of the Talmud, the 'Mishnah'. The Talmud text is completed in 500.

711   Muslims rule Spain, and Jewish life flourishes freely.

1040 - In France, Rabbi Shlomo ben Yitzhak ('Rashi') explains the Bible and
1105   Talmud in clear language. His commentaries are the most important in the Jewish world.

1135 - In Spain, Rabbi Moses ben Maimon ('The Rambam' or Maimonides)
1204   creates many works to explain Jewish laws and beliefs. These 'codes' are still used today.

1215 The Pope orders Jews in Europe to wear a yellow badge and an ugly hat so that Christians can recognize and avoid them. Over the next centuries, Jews are forced to live in closed areas, which become known as 'ghettos'.

'THE GOLDEN AGE OF SPAIN'

There were Jews in Spain from the first century CE. After Spain became Christian, during the Roman Empire, Jews were treated well at first, but they were severely persecuted under Christian rule from 612. In 711, Muslim Arabs conquered Spain and, although they did not see Jews as their equals, they treated them more fairly and respected them for their abilities. Jews spoke Arabic and some had important jobs in Spanish society, for example as doctors or translators. Jews had good relations with Muslims and were free to be themselves. This period is known as 'The Golden Age of Spain'. Soon after Spain became Christian again, in the twelfth century, Church leaders tried to convert Jews to Christianity. Many Jews were killed because they refused. Others kept their religion secretly and pretended to be Christian to save their lives. In 1492 Jews and Muslims were driven out of Spain.

Note:
BCE means Before the Common Era. CE means in the Common Era.
(See further explanation on page 47.)

TIMELINE OF THE JEWISH PEOPLE

1492   The Christian King and Queen of Spain expel Jews and Muslims.

1654   Jews settle in North America.

1700 - The 'Baal Shem Tov' ('Master of the Good Name') becomes the
1760   founder of the Hasidic movement in Poland. Hasidic Jews stress the joy of living a Jewish life, expressing this in song, story and dance. Reverence for the rabbi is very important.

1806   Napoleon encourages a Jewish assembly to be created in France, showing that Jews are equal to others: the beginning of the modern period, the 'Enlightenment'.

1810 - Abraham Geiger, a German rabbi, recommends many changes in
1874   Jewish practice. Reform Judaism dates from this time.

1881   'Pogroms', organized attacks on Jews, take place in Russia and neighbouring countries. Many Jews are killed or expelled, or emigrate – mainly to the USA.

The Shoah

The Holocaust is the most tragic of all the persecutions of Jews. Its Hebrew name, 'Shoah', means 'whirlwind'. The Nazis did not want Jews to become Christian or to change in any way. They wanted them dead and had a plan to make the world 'free of Jews'. They built concentration camps and killed six million Jews. This was almost all the Jews in Europe and about one-third of the Jewish population of the world at the time. Nazis also killed six million other people that they thought were 'sub-human', including gypsies, and the physically disabled and mentally ill.

Anne Frank's family hid from the Nazis in Holland, where Anne kept her diary. All but her father died in concentration camps.

1897 In Switzerland, Theodor Herzl convenes the First Zionist Congress, a big meeting of Jews to discuss ideas for a modern Jewish homeland in Israel.

1917 The British government issues the Balfour Declaration, promising the Jews a national homeland in Palestine.

1933 Nazis come to power in Germany.

1948 The State of Israel is created and declared as a homeland for all Jews. Refugees arrive. Surrounding countries declare war on Israel and capture the Old City of Jerusalem.

1967 The 'Six Day War': surrounding countries attack Israel. Israel captures the West Bank from Jordan and the Gaza Strip from Egypt. The Old and New Cities of Jerusalem are reunited.

1982 Israel signs a peace agreement with Egypt. The 'Peace Process' begins.

1994 Israel signs peace agreements with the Palestinians, and with Jordan. Palestinians begin limited self-rule in part of the West Bank and the Gaza Strip.

In concentration camps and on forced marches, Jews sang a Yiddish song, 'Zog Nit Keynmol' (Never Say You Walk the Final Way). It is often sung at services to remember those who died in the Shoah. Its first verse is:

We must never lose our courage
in the fight
though skies of lead turn days of
sunshine into night,
because the hour for which we've
yearn'd will yet arrive
and our marching steps will thunder:
we survive!

'The Silent Scream', a sculpture in the gardens of Yad V'Shem, a museum of the Shoah, in Israel. A Jewish visitor has left a stone in the folds of the figure's clothes, as when visiting a grave.

The past and the future

From every age, something lives on and can be seen and felt in Jewish life today. For Jews, the most important part of history is not the past but the future. They look forward rather than look back. They hope for a time of peace, justice and freedom for everyone which they call 'the days of the Messiah'. This verse is used in Jewish prayers and sums up this belief:

'I believe with perfect faith in the coming of the Messiah and, even though it takes a long time, I still believe.'

HER FATHER'S DAUGHTER

This real-life story shows how Jewish people feel about their history and identity. Alice was nine when she heard about Jews at school. She could not work out who they were, so her father told her about the Jewish people, from far back to the present day. She was fascinated by the fortunes of the Jewish people that go up and down, in and out... 'Are there any Jews alive now?' she asked. Her father replied that there were millions. Alice longed to meet Jews and discover how they survived. 'Do you know any Jews?' she asked. 'Yes... and so do you!' – 'Who? Who?' Desperate to know, she was angry with her father for only answering, 'One day you'll know...' A few months later, quite suddenly, he died. Years afterwards, she discovered that he was Jewish, although her mother was not. His family had suffered greatly because they were Jews, and many of them had been killed. Her mother had not wanted him or the family to suffer any more and had asked him to keep it a secret; he loved her very much and he agreed. Alice found out all she could about Jews. As a young woman, she became Jewish 'to remember what my father might have forgotten...'

2

THE WORLD OF JEWS

The Jewish people originated in the land of Israel, but now live all over the world. Jews do not try to convert people to their religion. They have spread mainly because they have been expelled from a country, or because it was hard to live a Jewish life there and they have chosen to leave.

In the nineteenth and twentieth centuries, many Jews emigrated to Israel. They see this as returning to Israel, and it is called 'aliyah' (going up). Some went to escape persecution; some wanted to return to the place where they feel that their people is meant to be; and some feel it is more natural for Jews to be together where they can be Jewish in everything they do. Some Jews could make aliyah but do not, because they think that they can support Israel better by living outside, or that being Jewish means having good relationships with other peoples – which would not happen so easily if every Jew lived in Israel.

Yosef Chernobilsky was born in 1984, in the former Soviet Union. His parents were 'refuseniks', Jews who were refused permission to leave the country. His father was imprisoned many times, for protesting against the Soviet authorities' cruel treatment of Jews and for asking to live in Israel. His mother taught Hebrew secretly, and was never caught. Quite suddenly, in 1990, the family were allowed to leave and now live in Israel. In the photograph, Yosef, aged 4, is playing with plastic Hebrew letters, a present from the West.

Left: A refugee arriving in Israel from the war-torn city of Sarajevo is reunited with a friend, who settled there two months before.

JEWISH POPULATIONS AROUND THE WORLD

In 1991 there were estimated to be 13,973,445 Jews in the world. The largest groups were in the USA, Israel and the former USSR.

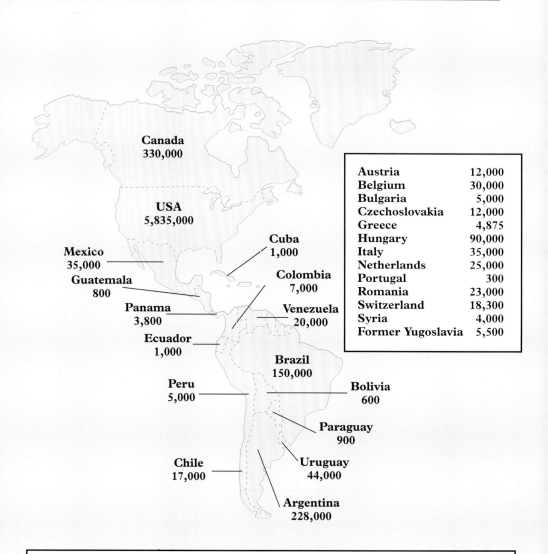

Canada
330,000

USA
5,835,000

Mexico
35,000

Guatemala
800

Panama
3,800

Ecuador
1,000

Cuba
1,000

Colombia
7,000

Venezuela
20,000

Brazil
150,000

Peru
5,000

Bolivia
600

Paraguay
900

Chile
17,000

Uruguay
44,000

Argentina
228,000

Austria	12,000
Belgium	30,000
Bulgaria	5,000
Czechoslovakia	12,000
Greece	4,875
Hungary	90,000
Italy	35,000
Netherlands	25,000
Portugal	300
Romania	23,000
Switzerland	18,300
Syria	4,000
Former Yugoslavia	5,500

DIFFERENT BUT SIMILAR

Sefardi and Ashkenazi Jews each have their own customs and pronounce Hebrew differently, but they practise their religion in very similar ways.

In Israel there are far more Sefardi than Ashkenazi Jews. Elsewhere, numbers of Sefardi and Ashkenazi Jews are more even.

ASHKENAZI JEWS

Jews whose families originate in northern, central and eastern Europe are known as 'Ashkenazi' Jews. Many Ashkenazi communities spoke a language called Yiddish for centuries. It is based on old German, with words from other languages, such as Polish, but is written in the Hebrew script. Small numbers of Jews still speak Yiddish and some Jews are trying to stop it dying out.

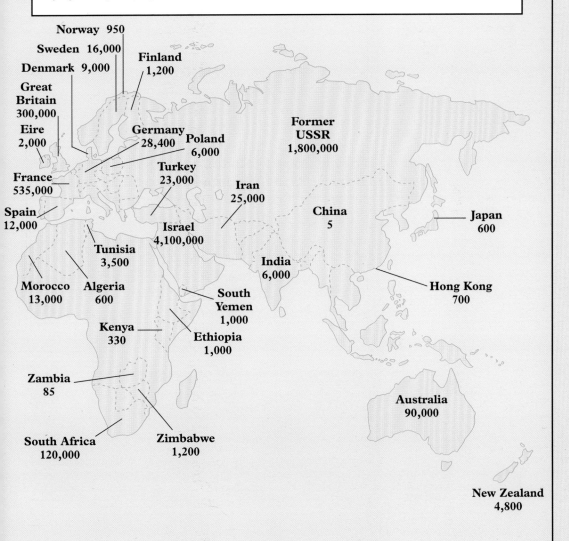

Norway 950
Sweden 16,000
Denmark 9,000
Finland 1,200
Great Britain 300,000
Eire 2,000
Germany 28,400
Poland 6,000
Former USSR 1,800,000
France 535,000
Turkey 23,000
Iran 25,000
China 5
Japan 600
Spain 12,000
Israel 4,100,000
India 6,000
Hong Kong 700
Tunisia 3,500
Morocco 13,000
Algeria 600
South Yemen 1,000
Kenya 330
Ethiopia 1,000
Zambia 85
Australia 90,000
South Africa 120,000
Zimbabwe 1,200
New Zealand 4,800

SEFARDI JEWS

Jews from southern Europe, the Middle East and further south are called 'Sefardi' Jews. Many Sefardi communities in southern Europe spoke a language called Ladino for centuries. It is very similar to old Spanish. Hardly any Jews speak Ladino today.

Jewish immigrants from Ethiopia are given temporary housing together for a while, where they learn Hebrew and get used to Israel's ways of life, before finding their own homes.

A LONG JOURNEY

In 1984, as the famine grew worse, the Berak family escaped from Ethiopia. As they travelled, bandits attacked them and stole their donkey, food and water. They became ill, but when someone died, they were too afraid to stop to bury him. They carried on, because it would be worse to turn back. Eventually they were put on a plane – the first they had ever seen – and taken to Israel. This was part of the Israeli rescue called 'Operation Moses'.

The Beraks were looked after in Israel, and learned Hebrew and how to use modern appliances. They found shops, buses, taps and electricity very strange at first. Moshe Berak says: 'Israeli life is so different. I don't think many people really understand our culture and this makes it hard to mix. In Ethiopia we were nicknamed "Falasha" – which means strangers – and people swore at us a lot. But we have always called ourselves "Beta Yisrael" – the House of Israel – and that is why I am glad to be in Israel, with my people.'

Young Jewish people at a holiday camp, run by the Women's International Zionist Organization.

3

JEWISH WRITINGS

'People of the book'

Jews are sometimes called 'the people of the book', because Jewish writings are so important to them. Many Jewish homes have lots of books – on Jewish and other subjects. Jews use the idea of 'speaking' and 'hearing' to express the way that they understand God. They do not mean that God really has a voice and ears, but that idea is the closest they come to describing how God and people communicate with each other. Jews feel that God is also expressed in the beauty of nature and in the love among people.

A young man in the Ukraine is immersed in the weekly Torah portion, and reads the text and commentaries from a 'humash'. The man in the background stands to say his morning prayers.

What is the Torah?

'Torah' is 'teaching' and the word is used in several ways. The 'Sefer Torah' is the first five books of the Bible, as a scroll or book. Torah also means all the

SAYINGS ABOUT THE TORAH

- The Torah speaks in a language all people understand.

- The Torah is like a good friend.

- The Torah sheds its grace on those who study it.

- The Torah can only be learned among friends.

- The Torah is deeper than the sea.

- The Torah is Light.

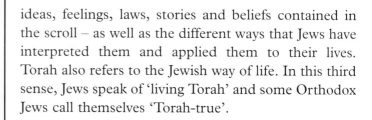

One of the most important sayings in the Torah is: 'Be holy for I, the Lord your God, am holy... Love your neighbour as yourself: I am the Lord.'
(*Leviticus 19: 2, 18*)

ideas, feelings, laws, stories and beliefs contained in the scroll – as well as the different ways that Jews have interpreted them and applied them to their lives. Torah also refers to the Jewish way of life. In this third sense, Jews speak of 'living Torah' and some Orthodox Jews call themselves 'Torah-true'.

Stories and sayings

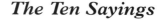

The Torah has many stories about the children of Israel, and the way they hear God speaking to them through their experiences and relationships. Some of the stories are about everyday things or normal family life, but some of the events and experiences are special to the children of Israel.

The Ten Sayings

The Torah contains 613 commandments through which God speaks to the children of Israel about how to worship and how to live. Not all the commandments apply to everyone, all the time. Some apply only in Israel and those to do with the temple do not apply at all today.

The most important commandments are 'the Ten Sayings'. Most synagogues have these clearly written, in Hebrew, on a wall plaque. Usually just the first phrase of each Saying is given, and often the first five and second five Sayings are shown as two lists, on two stones or sheets. This reminds Jews of the tradition that Moses received the Ten Sayings, written on two stones or tablets, on Mount Sinai.

The US-born artist Philip Ratner has depicted the Ten Sayings in ten paintings. 'You shall not commit adultery' (top) shows features of the wedding ceremony. The four angels hold the canopy. 'Respect your father and mother so that the days of your life be fulfilled' is shown as a series of generations in a family.

Understanding the Torah

Traditionally, Jews have thought of the Torah as a letter from God, but some Orthodox and most Conservative, as well as most Progressive, Jews today see the influence of people in the creation of the Torah. They think that the Torah was passed on by word of mouth for a long time, before it was written down. But, however Jews understand the Torah, they all use exactly the same text.

Sefardi Jews in Middle Eastern countries traditionally have a wooden or metal case for the Torah. This boy has become Bar Mitzvah and is reading during the morning service at the Western Wall.

Written and oral Torah

By the time of the exile in Babylon, at least part of the Torah had been written down and was being read to the people. They discussed what it meant, and wise people explained it to them. By the time of the rabbis, these discussions became very important and are called the oral Torah. This was remembered and eventually written down, to form the 'Talmud' (study). Traditional Jews believe that the oral Torah was given to Moses at the same time as the written Torah, but took many hundreds of years to be discovered through discussion.

WAYS OF SEEING THE TORAH

There are several ways to see the Torah and how it came to the Jewish people:

A letter from God:
God spoke the Torah directly to Moses, Moses wrote it down completely and exactly, and no word of the Torah has ever changed or can ever change.

A telephone message from God:
The *ideas* of the Torah were given to Moses and he wrote them down in human words.

A diary of the people:
The Torah was created by people who believed in God and recorded their experiences.

A holiday scrap book:
The Torah is put together as it goes along and contains different kinds of material, including records of later thoughts.

'If I am not for myself, who will be for me? But if I am only for myself, what am I? And, if not now, when?' (Hillel)

'You do not have to finish the work but you are not free to neglect it!' (Tarfon)

'Who is wise? The one who learns from everyone. Who is strong? The one who controls themself. Who is rich? The one who is happy with what they have. Who is honourable? The one who honours others.' (Ben Zoma)

A silver yad.

Pirkei Avot

The Talmud is a large collection of books. One of the best-known is the 'Pirkei Avot' ('Chapters of the Ancestors' or 'Sayings of the Fathers'), which is made up of short sayings. In most of the Talmud, people who had particular ideas are not named, but in the Pirkei Avot they are. Some of the sayings have been set to music and are loved by Jewish young people.

Reading the Torah

Reading the Torah is a regular part of Jewish community worship. There is a portion of the Torah for each week and, in a year, the whole Torah is read from beginning to end. There are also portions for festivals.

The Torah is always read in Hebrew from a scroll, exactly as it is written. As the letters are close together, a pointer called a 'yad' (hand) helps the reader to follow the text, without risking smudging the writing. A Torah scroll is always written by hand, by a trained scribe, who takes enormous care to make the lines straight and even. Sometimes the scribe has to make letters near the end of a line large, to ensure that the words fill the line.

TeNaKh

The Jewish Bible is made up of the **T**orah, the **N**evi'im (prophets, such as Jeremiah), and the **K**etuvim ('Writings', including the Psalms). The initials of the three parts make 'TeNaKh', which is the name for the Jewish Bible. A part of the Nevi'im is read after every weekly Torah portion. Parts of the Ketuvim are read at certain festivals, and psalms are sung all the time.

The TeNaKh is almost the same as the Christian Old Testament, but Jews do not like that name for their Bible because, to them, it is not old but always fresh, alive and eternal.

The Torah is the life and soul of the party on Simhat Torah and occasions such as the completion of writing a scroll.

LOVING THE TORAH

When the Romans occupied the land of Israel, in the first century CE, they forbade Jews to study the Torah, on pain of death. Rabbi Akiva told this parable:

'A fox called to a fish, from the river bank, "It must be very cold and dark in there. There are stones on the bottom and the water gets rough in places. But up here, it's lovely. Why don't you get out and we can play together?" The fish knew she could not survive out of water and that the fox was trying to trick her. So she replied, "I like my river and it's my home. It's hard for me to live in a place I know, but it would be even harder to live in a place I don't know!" And she swam away.

Rabbi Akiva said that the fox was like the Romans, the fish like the Jews and the river like the Torah. It may be hard for Jews to live with the Torah when the Romans were there, but it would be even harder without the Torah. Jewish life can only survive *with* the Torah.

This midrash is one of the oldest and is well known by Jewish children. It explores how Abraham turned away from idol worship:

Abraham's father was an idol merchant and left him in charge of the shop one day. Abraham looked at all the statues, of different sizes and materials, took a large hammer and smashed them one by one – all but the very biggest. His father was furious with him but Abraham pointed to the big idol and said, 'That one did it!'

'Don't be stupid!' replied his father. 'It couldn't possibly... Idols have no power!'

'Then why do you worship them?'

Humash

Few individual Jews have a Torah scroll, but many have a 'humash'. This is a book of the weekly portions of the Torah, with a translation and explanation of each one, and the reading from the Nevi'im that goes with it. Jews always study the Torah with a commentary – notes written by learned people in the past and present. In this way, they are part of the ongoing tradition of the Torah – and not just individuals trying to understand what it means on their own. Many Jews in synogogue follow the Torah reading from a humash.

All Jews are encouraged to take time each day to study and pray. Many synagogues create an informal atmosphere where people can feel at ease. The seating in this Tunisian synagogue makes it easy to get comfortable and this elderly Jew can relax with a book.

Midrash

A 'midrash' (searching) is a story to explain and explore something in the Bible. Midrashim (plural) developed at about the same time as the Talmud and were recorded in books. Jews go on making midrashim all the time.

4

THE JEWISH HOME

Home is important to Jews. Events in a person's life and all festivals are celebrated or commemorated at home, and the synagogue takes second place. It is mostly through the home that children learn about their religion, history and culture. They learn by doing Jewish things, such as touching the mezuzah at the door to their home and kissing their fingers, putting coins into the charity box, helping to prepare for Shabbat and, more formally, discussing texts, especially at meal-times.

In many homes, Jews put money into a charity box before Shabbat and festivals. Ester Gluck's family collects for tree-planting in Israel.

LEARNING AND LIVING

Ester Gluck is twelve years old. Like many Jewish children, she cannot remember when she learned she was Jewish. It seems as if she always knew it.

Ester has kept the mezuzah-kissing custom since she was a toddler. One day, on reaching home, she cried, 'Kiss 'zuzah!' and insisted on being lifted up – even though her mother had armfuls of shopping and was rummaging for her keys!

When it was her turn at nursery school to bring home the rabbits for the winter holidays, Ester learned the Talmudic teaching that Jews should feed their animals before themselves. So every morning she marched out into the snow to give the rabbits cabbage – and then had her own breakfast.

Ester knew the blessing for bread when she was only two. 'What really matters,' her mother says, 'is whether she still says it when she's twenty-two and whether she teaches it to her children when they're two!'

THE SHEMA

The reason why the Shema is put on doorposts is given in the Shema itself:

'Hear, O Israel, the Lord is our God. The Lord is one. Love the Lord your God with all your heart, and with all your soul and with all your might. These words that I command you today shall be upon your heart. Repeat them to your children, and talk about them when you sit in your home, and when you walk in the street; when you lie down and when you rise up. Hold fast to them as a sign upon your hand, and let them be as reminders before your eyes. Write them at the doorposts of your home and at your gates.'
(Deuteronomy 6: 4 – 9)

The mezuzah

On the door of a Jewish home, there is a mezuzah, a tiny box containing a piece of scroll. In it are written the words of the 'Shema', which is one of the most important passages in the Torah and a prayer recited evening and morning. The custom of touching the mezuzah and kissing the fingers, on the way in and out, is a sign of love for what the writing means and the value of the home.

The Old City of Jerusalem is walled, with eight gates, and in many ways it is like a huge home. A tourist pauses at the Jaffa Gate to touch the mezuzah and kiss her fingers.

The table

Modern life affects Jews as much as others and they, too, may have stand-up breakfasts in the kitchen or TV suppers. Most Jewish families try to eat together at least once a day and always on Shabbat. Observant Jews say a blessing over food to show that they are grateful to God and others for what they are able to eat. For instance the blessing for bread is: 'Blessed are you, Lord our God, ruler of the universe, who brings forth bread from the earth.'

Kashrut – rules about food

There are rules about what Jews may eat, called 'kashrut' by Sefardi Jews, and 'kashrus' by Ashkenazi Jews. Food which Jews are allowed to eat is called 'kasher' or 'kosher' (meaning 'proper' or 'fit'). Orthodox Jews observe the laws about food strictly, at home and when out. For Progressive Jews, they are less important and some may observe them only partly, for example, just by not eating pork or shellfish. Today many Jews 'keep kosher' at home, but not completely when out with non-Jewish friends.

Meat, milk and other foods

Birds and mammals must be killed with a single, swift cut, by a trained 'shohet' (slaughterer), who cares about the animals' feelings and about Jewish laws. Meat which has not been prepared like this is called 'tref' (torn or strangled). 'Tref' is also used for all food which is not kasher.

To make the meat kasher, the blood must be removed by soaking, salting and rinsing. This is because the blood is thought to contain the animal's life-essence. Kashering the meat can be done by the butcher or by someone at home.

Meat and milk must not be eaten together. This comes from a verse in the Torah, 'Do not stew a kid in its mother's milk', and reminds Jews of the feelings between the mother and her baby. Meat symbolizes death and milk symbolizes life and so they are not mixed. Orthodox Jews have separate sets of crockery and cutlery for milk and meat foods.

Most foods are neither milk nor meat, and are called 'parev' or 'parve'. They include eggs, fish and food from plants. Jews can eat parev food with meat or with milk or by itself.

Kashrut is complicated in the modern world because there are so many processed foods with additives which may be tref. Some Jewish food producers ask a

KASHRUT

Kashrut is like a formula rather than a list of foods. For example, Jews may eat:

 fish that have fins and scales. So cod is kasher, but prawns are not.

 the meat of birds that eat grain, but not birds of prey. So chickens are kasher, but owls are not.

 the meat of mammals which have split hooves and chew their cud. So sheep are kasher, but pigs are not.

 any edible plants, the milk of kasher animals and the eggs of kasher birds.

rabbi to supervise production, to certify that the food is kasher, so that Jews will feel able to eat it. Rabbis also analyse other products and issue lists of brand names which are kasher. Orthodox Jews refer to these lists when shopping. In Israel, 'keeping kosher' is easy, because most food shops stock only kasher products.

In most homes, Jews stand to sing 'kiddush' (a prayer) on Shabbat. The white table cloth symbolizes the Shabbat as a bride. This family has the custom of singing kiddush with one cup of wine, which the father holds. He then pours a little wine into each cup for the family and guests.

Men and women

Men and women play different roles in Jewish ritual. For example, the woman usually lights candles for Shabbat, but the man says the blessing over the bread. Men's and women's roles are valued equally. At home, either or both may cook, polish the candlesticks for Shabbat, or bath the baby, and both may contribute to the family income.

Parents and children

One of the Ten Sayings is 'Honour your father and mother', but there is no saying 'Honour your children'. One explanation is that parents instinctively respect and love their children, but it does not come naturally to children to respect and love their parents – and so they have to be told to!

It is the last night of Hanukah. All eight candles and the 'shammas' candle in the 'hanukiyah' (candle holder) have been lit, and it is time for a familiar festival story. The shammas (helper or servant) candle is used to light all the others.

FROM GENERATION TO GENERATION

This midrash is about parents and children, and the need to care for future generations:

As the rain fell heavily and the waters rose, a family of birds was afraid of drowning in the flood. So the father bird flew with his young on his back – one at a time – from their nest to a dry place. Half-way across, he asked the first baby, 'When I am old, will you care for me as I care for you?' The baby answered, 'Yes, of course, father!' This was not the answer he hoped for – and he dropped the little bird into the water below. He asked the second one the same question, got the same answer – and did the same thing. Half-way across, he asked the third, 'When I am old, will you care for me as I care for you?' This one replied, 'I don't know, father... but I hope I shall care for *my* children as you care for me!' The father carried his baby lovingly to a new nest.

THE JEWISH COMMUNITY

This joke shows how important synagogues are – and that Jewish humour is often self-mocking. A Jew who had been stranded on a desert island showed his rescuers what he had done. 'Here's the house I built and the synagogue. That's the one I go to...' They asked, 'Why have you made a second synagogue?' He replied, 'That's the one I wouldn't be seen dead in!'

Home is so important in the Jewish tradition that the synagogue, the main community institution, is called 'a house'. It has three Hebrew names and each conveys one of its uses. Many North American Jews call the synagogue 'the temple'.

A house of gathering

In Israel, 'bet knesset' (house of gathering) is the most common name. Synagogues all round the world are used for many activities, such as parties, fund-raising events, meetings of voluntary workers, day centres for the elderly or disabled, and toddler groups. Most synagogues have a kitchen and toilets, and many have offices where the synagogue's work is organized.

Some young Jewish people go to the synagogue during the week for classes given by their rabbi.

A house of learning

Yiddish-speaking Jews call the synagogue 'shul' (school). The Hebrew name as pronounced by Sefardi Jews is 'bet midrash' and by Ashkenazi Jews 'bes midrash'. This name means 'house of study'.

Synagogues provide many opportunities for Jews to learn. The most important is the weekly reading of the Torah. This may be followed by a sermon given by the rabbi or another member of the congregation. A sermon is called a 'derasha', which is another form of the 'study' word.

Shabbat, which lasts from Friday evening to Saturday evening, is the most important time of the week, and more Jews go to synagogue then than on weekdays. Shabbat is a rest-day, when Jews study by reading and talking. For observant Jews, resting includes not writing, using computers, painting, cutting, sticking... So religion classes for children and young people are usually held on Sundays (and possibly after school).

Most synagogues offer classes for adults, on topics from reading Hebrew to baking bread. Progressive synagogues, in particular, create opportunities for families to learn together informally through games, quizzes and drama activities. These often take the form of a 'Family Day'.

'A Lifeline to the Aged' is a workshop programme in Israel through which retired people can learn and develop skills, talk to others of their age group, and earn money when what they make is sold. This man learned pottery and says that 'a whole world opened up to him'.

A GREAT LAUGH

Desi Tammam's family is Sefardi, from Libya, and lives in Britain. Desi is in her late teens. She says: 'A youth group is held in the "House" where there are activities for age groups 4 to 25 – all sorts of role plays and discussions, about the Holocaust or Soviet Jews and how we feel when we get called names in the street. There are holiday camps, too. The youngest children sleep in buildings, but the teenagers are in tents. It's a great laugh!'

In Orthodox synagogues, men and women study separately; in Progressive synagogues, they study together. In recent years, more women have studied together than before. When Moses was on Mount Sinai receiving the Torah, the men became impatient and wanted to make a golden calf to worship as an idol – but the women refused to contribute their jewellery! The New Moon became a 'women's festival' as their reward for not worshipping idols. The celebration died away, but some women are reviving it. They meet for study, as well as prayer, song and the sharing of food.

A house of prayer

Another Hebrew name for the synagogue is 'bet t'filah' (house of prayer). The Hebrew for 'prayer' comes from a word meaning 'to judge oneself'. Jews may pray alone, but are encouraged to pray with other Jews. This does not need to be in a synagogue. Most prayers say 'we', 'us' and 'our', rather than 'I', 'me' and 'my' – and 'you' when addressing God. A 'minyan' is a group of ten or more adult males, the number traditionally required for a service to be 'public'. If there is no minyan, Orthodox Jews leave out some

The Torah is carried round the synagogue, as the congregation sings psalms. Many people come close, to touch it with the fringes of their prayer shawl. An Ashkenazi scroll has a removable velvet cover. The bells jingle softly so that everyone can hear as well as see it.

prayers from their service. This rule encourages Orthodox Jews to want to join in the service, because they are needed. Progressive communities do not count a minyan.

The rabbi and the hazan

Some synagogues do not have a rabbi; some synagogues have more than one rabbi; and some rabbis work in more than one synagogue. Nowadays, rabbis are paid for the work they do and most do not have other jobs. Rabbis are ordained to teach and to judge, but they also give people advice with problems and comfort them when they are troubled. In Orthodox communities, only men can become rabbis. Some Progressive and Conservative rabbis are women.

Most Orthodox and Conservative communities have a 'hazan', a trained singer who leads the sung parts of the prayers and often chants the Torah portion. Many Progressive communities have choirs of men and women. Orthodox choirs are less common and are always male.

'Know before whom you stand' is the inscription over the Ark in this British Orthodox synagogue. Above it are the Ten Sayings. Usually the 'bimah' (platform) is in the middle of the congregation and faces the Ark, although here it is at the front. In most synagogues, as here, there are seats at the side so that people face in and can see each other. This gives a feeling of oneness.

THE SIDDUR

The siddur (prayer book) was first compiled in the eighth century and is still developing. Its structure is the same throughout the Jewish world, with variations. For example, some Sefardi prayer books include Ladino prayers, and Progressive prayer books do not refer to temple sacrifices.

'God said "Let there be light" and there was light....God called the light day and he called the darkness night...' has been written here by artist and scribe Gordon Charatan. He rounded the Hebrew letters at the ends of each line, to make the circle.

Services

The Jewish day begins at sunset and has three services: evening, morning and afternoon. These come from the times when priests offered sacrifices in the temple. On Shabbat and festivals, there is an additional service after the morning service.

In Orthodox synagogues, the weekly Torah portion is read on Monday, Thursday and Saturday mornings; in Progressive synagogues, only on Saturday mornings.

The Prayer Book, called the 'siddur' (order), contains Psalms and prayers from the Bible, as well as later compositions. It is mostly in Hebrew, sometimes with a translation into the everyday language. In Progressive and some Conservative services, some of the prayers are said in translation.

In Orthodox synagogues, men and women sit separately and children may sit with either. Women are usually upstairs or behind a screen. In Progressive synagogues, men, women and children sit together. Some Conservative synagogues have separate seating, and others mixed.

6

THE LIFETIME OF A JEW

Welcoming a baby

When a Jewish boy is eight days old, he is circumcised. A 'mohel', a specially trained person, who is often a Jewish doctor or surgeon, removes the foreskin of the boy's penis. As the baby's nervous system is not fully developed, the pain is far less than it would be for an older boy. This simple ritual often takes place in the home and is accompanied by a party. The Torah commands Jewish fathers to have their sons circumcised, to show that they have entered the covenant, or promise, of Abraham. The celebration of this commandment is called 'brit milah' (the covenant of cutting). Family and friends say, 'Just as he has entered into the covenant, so may he also enter into the blessings of Torah, of marriage and of good deeds.'

Jewish parents name a new baby after a member of their family or someone in Jewish history, or they choose a name which points to qualities that they hope the child will grow up to have. In Ashkenazi custom, children are named after dead relatives, but in Sefardi custom they can be named after living relatives.

Jews have a Hebrew name, which is used in many Jewish rituals and appears in Jewish documents. Their Hebrew name is used when they are called to the Torah, married and buried. Outside Israel, Jews also have an 'everyday' name which may be quite different from their Hebrew name.

A brit milah in a synagogue. There is more room than in a home and the occasion becomes a community event.

Parents also take their baby to synagogue to announce its name. The community welcomes the new member.

This is part of a prayer said by Progressive Jewish girls. There is also a version for Bar Mitzvah.

'... I now prepare to take upon myself the duties which are binding on all the family of Israel... I think of those who have gone before me, who through all the troubles of the world preserved this heritage of holiness and goodness, so that I should enter into it now. May I be a true Bat Mitzvah... May I be a witness to the living God and his goodness, and the tradition that lives within me.'

A Bat Mitzvah-to-be, encouraged by her rabbi, reads the Torah text for the last time before chanting it to the congregation the following morning.

Growing up

In the Jewish tradition, girls are considered adult at the age of twelve and boys at thirteen. These young adults are responsible for their actions and are expected to obey the commandments. Since the Middle Ages, the custom has developed of marking the stage when a boy becomes a man by inviting him to lead the congregation in prayer, or to read the weekly Torah portion. He is called 'Bar Mitzvah' (son of the commandment). It has become a big event, especially in North America.

A blessing is pronounced as a boy becomes Bar Mitzvah.

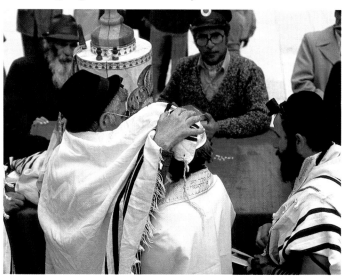

In 1923, in a Progressive synagogue in New York, a girl was called to the Torah for the first time as 'Bat Mitzvah' (daughter of the commandment). Since then, many Progressive Jewish girls have celebrated becoming Bat Mitzvah in the same way as boys.

Orthodox Jewish girls have also begun to celebrate coming of age, but in a different way from Progressive girls and boys, and Orthodox boys. Usually, the name given is 'Bat Hayil' (daughter of valour) and a group of girls have a joint celebration at which they read psalms and poetry. It is not part of a normal service, but a separate occasion.

The final run-through for the big day. Tomorrow Libby will be Bat Mitzvah and take her place in the congregation as a Jewish woman.

A SPECIAL DAY AT A SPECIAL TIME

Solomon Sananes comes from a large, close-knit Egyptian Sefardi family. 'I was Bar Mitzvah in 1967. It was a year of tough studying, but we managed to lark about, too! It was nerve-racking going up to the "bimah" (platform), even though I had had a run-through the day before. Family came from far and wide and we had an open house straight after the service for the rabbi, relatives and friends. The main function was on the Sunday evening. I was perhaps too young and overwhelmed to take it in – but it was a very happy occasion. Some people gave my parents a bit of flak, saying that all the money they spent should have gone to Israel, because of the Six Day War three months earlier. But my parents felt that what they gave to charity was their business, that joyous events are important in Jewish life, and that they could support Israel *and* celebrate their son's Bar Mitzvah.'

Marriage

The Jewish wedding ceremony is basically simple and is a combination of two ceremonies: the betrothal and the marriage. Customs throughout the world make the ceremony beautiful, interesting and more complex. But it is first of all a binding agreement between the man and the woman, and there need to be two witnesses. The man gives the wife a 'ketubah' (marriage contract), which states that he will look after her, in the event of divorce or death. To show that she is willing to marry him, the woman points the index finger of her right hand and he puts a ring on it, saying, 'By this ring, you are married to me in holiness according to the law of Moses and of Israel.'

The wedding takes place under a 'huppah' (canopy), which symbolizes the openness of the home. The ceremony itself is called 'huppah v'kiddushin' (canopy and holiness). Ideally, the huppah is outside, but can also be in a home or synagogue. The bride is usually veiled

The ketubah is a binding legal agreement and often a work of art too. The round shape symbolizes the eternity of love, and the motif here is the walls of Jerusalem. The ketubah becomes the bride's property, and she will probably frame and hang it at home.

at first, but her veil is lifted as she is 'revealed' to her husband. The couple share wine. A hazan, choir or friends sing seven blessings, which include: 'Give these companions in love great happiness, the happiness of your creatures in Eden long ago. Blessed are you, Lord, who rejoices the bridegroom and the bride.'

At the end of the ceremony, the husband 'smashes a glass with his foot. This symbolizes the destruction of the temple, which shattered the Jewish people. It also reminds Jews that life is fragile and that even happy moments can be tinged with sadness. When they hear the broken glass, all the guests shout 'Mazal tov!' (Good luck!)

David Gryn painted this vibrant yet intimate picture of a bride and groom as a gift for his sister when she got married.

Death and mourning

When someone dies, those who knew and loved him or her are encouraged to express their feelings. Men and women are allowed to cry freely. Jews think it is silly to try to be brave when you are feeling sad. Many of the customs around Jewish funerals are meant to help people grieve, and also help them gradually back to life without the one who died.

Jewish funerals take place as soon as possible after death, usually on the same or the following day. This means that grieving can start quickly. Most Jews are buried, but some Progressive Jews are cremated.

The dead person is washed and carefully wrapped in a white garment. Some men are also dressed in their 'tallit' (prayer shawl). Sometimes the body is placed in a coffin for burial and sometimes it is placed directly in the ground. Close mourners often throw the first

THE KADDISH

This prayer does not mention death at all, but praises God as the giver of life: 'Let us magnify and let us sanctify the great name of God in the world which he created according to his will. May his kingdom come in your lifetime, and in your days, and in the lifetime of the family of Israel – quickly and speedily may it come... He is far beyond any blessing or song, any honour or any consolation that can be spoken of in this world.'

shovelfuls of soil into the grave and this helps them to feel that their loved one is really dead. A cemetery is called 'bet hayim' (house of life) or 'bet olam' (house of eternity). As people leave, they may wash their hands, to symbolize that they are leaving death behind and are beginning to return to the world of life.

For a week, friends and family meet to comfort each other and say prayers in the home of the person who has died. Close family do not have to go to work or school for a week and cannot be expected to do anything. The idea is that people need to grieve without worrying about anything else and grieving makes people tired. Friends and relatives do whatever the mourners need.

When visiting a Jewish grave to remember and pay respect to the dead, it is a custom to leave a small stone as a mark of the visit and a sign of the harsh reality of death.

For almost a year, close mourners recite the 'kaddish' (holy prayer) every day. Within a year of the death, the gravestone is erected. Sefardi gravestones lie flat over the grave, to show that in death everyone is equal. Ashkenazi gravestones are flat or upright. On every anniversary of death, close mourners recite the kaddish and light a candle that burns all night and day.

7

THE JEWISH YEAR

Through the year, festivals help Jews to experience and express many customs and emotions. The main festivals are shown on the chart on the next page.

The Jewish calendar

The Jewish calendar is made up of natural months, which last from new moon to new moon. In ancient times, a month began when a new moon was sighted in Jerusalem. However, for centuries, Jewish scholars have calculated when new moons would come. Lunar months are 29 or 30 days long, so there are twelve and a bit in a year. To use the extra days and keep festivals in their season, some years have a 'leap month'.

Before the new moon could be calculated, Jews outside Israel did not know when it would come, so they celebrated it on two days. They also observed the festivals given in the Torah for two days – except Yom Kippur. Orthodox Jews outside Israel keep the tradition of double-day celebrations, but Progressive Jews keep just one day, like Israeli Jews.

Apples dipped in honey are eaten at Rosh Hashanah.

A family in their 'sukkah' for the festival of Sukkot. The father holds the 'four species', including the sweet-smelling yellow 'etrog'.

THE MOST WIDELY CELEBRATED

English and Hebrew Names	Time	What the festival remembers, or how it began
Passover Pesah	7/8 days in March/April	The Israelites' escape from slavery in Egypt.
Holocaust Day Yom HaShoah	1 day in April	The destruction of 6 million Jews and thousands of communities by the Nazis during the Holocaust. Day of memorial decreed by the Israeli parliament.
Israel Independence Day Yom HaAtzmaut	1 day in April/May	The creation of the State of Israel.
Pentecost Shavuot	1/2 days in June	The giving of the Torah to Moses on Mount Sinai.
Ninth of Av Tisha B'Av	1 day in August	The destruction of the first temple and the second temple – and other Jewish tragedies.
New Year Rosh Hashanah	1/2 days in September	Newness. A day of blowing the shofar (ram's horn).
Day of Atonement Yom Kippur	1 day in September/October	Repentance. Before the destruction of the second temple, the high priest made atonement for people on this day.
Booths/Tabernacles Sukkot	7/8 days in September/October	The children of Israel building booths in the wilderness.
8th day of Sukkot/ Rejoicing in Torah Shemini Atzeret/Simhat Torah	1/2 days in September/October	The 8th day is given in the Torah, but the Simhat Torah celebration developed in the Middle Ages as a finale to Sukkot.
Festival of Dedication Hanukah	8 days in December	Restoration of temple worship by the Maccabees, after it had been spoiled by enemy idol-worshippers.
New Year of Trees Tu B'Shevat	1 day in January	Care for the environment. Dating from the Talmudic period, it marks the time when fruit of trees begins to form.
Festival of Lots Purim	1 day in February/March	Ester, Jewish wife of king of Persia, risking her life to save her people from a tyrant, Haman.

☐ Given in the Torah   ☐ Modern
☐ Decreed by Jewish leaders in ancient times

FESTIVALS AND FASTS IN THE JEWISH YEAR

Day of rest?	How Jews celebrate
First and last days	No foods containing leaven are eaten and Jews eat matzah instead of ordinary bread. A Seder (Passover supper) is held on the 1st/2nd evening, with songs and stories from a book called the 'Haggadah' (Telling). Symbolic foods evoke the experience of captivity and freedom.
No	Especially important in Israel and among North American and European Jews. Jews gather to remember, mourn and strengthen themselves to prevent such tragedies in the future. Readings from Holocaust literature, specially composed prayers, singing songs from the Holocaust period.
No, but a public holiday in Israel	Public parades and parties in Israel and parties in Jewish communities elsewhere, with Israeli food and songs, including the Israeli national anthem, 'HaTikvah' (Hope).
Yes	Studying – all night by some people. Eating dairy foods, decorating homes and synagogues with flowers. Reading Torah, including the Ten Sayings.
No	Reading the Book of Lamentations. Fasting completely for a day – including not wearing leather.
Yes	Blowing the shofar for spiritual awakening. Synagogue cloths in white and some people in white clothes. Eating apples and honey, honey cakes and 'new' fruits. Sending New Year cards. Asking forgiveness for past year, before Yom Kippur.
Yes	Total fast for 25 hours. Lighting candles at home which burn for 25 hours. Congregation in synagogue make confessions to God. Synagogue cloths in white and white clothes worn by some people. Blowing shofar at end of fast.
First day(s)	Families and communities build sukkot (temporary, fragile huts) and live in them for a week. Four symbolic plants are used. Shaking the lulav (date palm).
Yes	Living in sukkot, but not shaking the lulav. Parading Torah scrolls in synagogues and in the streets. Reading the end and the beginning of the Torah, because the Torah is continuous.
No	Lighting candles each night for eight nights – one on first night, two on second night... Eating foods cooked in oil, such as latkes (potato pancakes) and doughnuts. Playing a game with a dreidl (special spinning top).
No, but special events in Israeli schools	Planting saplings in Israel. Outside Israel, tasting 15 fruits.
No, but school holiday in Israel	Reading the Book of Ester and trying to make enough noise to drown out the name of Haman. Wearing fancy dress. Eating hamantashen (triangular, filled sweet pastries).

This Yemeni family at Pesah time has set out the Matzah and the symbolic foods for the Seder. The bone and burnt egg recall sacrifices in the temple. A paste of nuts, dates, apples and wine, called 'haroset', is a reminder of the mortar the slaves used on building works in Egypt. Cos lettuce and radishes represent bitterness. Vinegar is for sadness and suffering. A green vegetable symbolizes springtime and hope.

A WARM GLOW

Samuel Gilmore is almost ninety. His family lived in Poland for centuries, then moved to London to escape persecution, but has now lived in the USA for many years. He says: 'My daughter holds a Seder for about fifteen friends and family. There are two Jewish mothers: my wife and my daughter! I take the first part of the haggadah and my son the second, but everybody has something to read. We all join in the singing too. There's a burst of enthusiasm which is what Jewish life should be. The Seder ends on a note of joy, with the hope that next year we'll be together in the same spirit...

'On Friday nights, in her home, my daughter says the prayers over the candles, which cast a warm glow over the whole household. The children and grandchildren are together and I have a great feeling of closeness. What more can an old Jew ask?'

Shabbat

The most important festival of all is Shabbat, a day for peace and rest which comes every week. The way other festivals are observed 'copies' Shabbat observance in many ways.

During the week, in preparation for Shabbat, Jews buy food they will need and clean the house thoroughly. On Friday, families come home in time to get ready and put the final touches to the food and table.

Traditionally, the table is set with a white cloth, two or more candles, wine or grape juice, and one or more special glasses or cups for 'kiddush' (a prayer over wine, on the themes of creation and freedom). There will also be two loaves of bread called 'hallah', which are made of a special dough and often plaited, a cover for the hallah, salt, and usually flowers, as well.

The theme of Shabbat is the God-Torah-Israel relationship and the plaited loaves symbolize this. Shabbat has three phases, each with a meal and each emphasizing one of the strands. On Friday evening, the theme is 'Israel', with friends and family enjoying each other's company and relaxing at the end of the week. The mood is light-hearted and the songs sung during the meal are happy ones. On Saturday morning there is the Torah reading at synagogue, which Jews often discuss over lunch. The afternoon is the 'God'-time, when the feeling is more private. Jews go for a walk, read, take a nap, talk quietly or just think personal thoughts...

When Shabbat is over on Saturday evening, the havdalah service marks the separation of rest and work and takes Jews back into the working week. As fire symbolizes work, havdalah begins with the lighting of a plaited candle. The candle again brings together the three themes of Shabbat. A box of sweet spices is passed around and sniffed, so that the fragrance and sweetness of Shabbat may linger, and there is wine for gladness. There is a legend that the prophet Elijah will return to herald the days of the Messiah when the world will be at peace. The final song yearns for him to come soon and to bring forever the day that has just been glimpsed on Shabbat. Then everyone wishes each other 'Shavua Tov!' – 'Have a good week!'

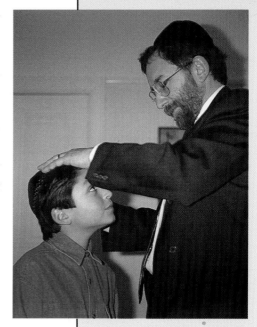

'May God make you like Ephraim and Manasseh' – two sons of Jacob. As a father blesses his son on a Friday evening, he wishes him all that is good.

Havdalah can be made at any time after Shabbat until Tuesday evening. These young people, meeting for Jewish classes on a Sunday morning, start with havdalah and wish each other a good week.

Glossary

aliyah	'going up': emigrating to Israel; being called to read the Torah.
Ashkenazi	originating in northern and eastern Europe.
Bar Mitzvah	'son of the commandment': a boy who is thirteen years old.
Bat Mitzvah	'daughter of the commandment': a girl who is twelve years old or, in a Progressive community, usually, thirteen.
brit milah	circumcision: marking a boy's entry into the covenant with God.
Conservative	a form of Judaism, especially in North America, which has features both of Reform and of Orthodox Judaism.
Hasidic	literally, 'pious'. The Hasidic movement began in Poland in the eighteenth century and emphasized purity of heart and joyous devotion to the Torah.
havdalah	'separation'; a ceremony to mark the end of Shabbat.
hazan	a trained singer who leads services, especially in Orthodox and Conservative synagogues.
Hebrew	the ancient and modern language which unifies the Jewish people; the language of the Torah and prayer books; the everyday language of Israel.
humash	a book containing the text of the Torah, with commentaries.
Israel	the homeland of the Jewish people since ancient times; a name for the Jewish people.
Jerusalem	the capital city of Israel. It is also called 'Zion', after the hill on which it was built.
kashrut	Jewish food laws. Food that Jews may eat is called 'kasher' or 'kosher'.
ketubah	a marriage document which the bridegroom gives to the bride.
kosher	See 'kashrut'.
Liberal	See 'Progressive' and 'Reform'.
Messiah	'the anointed one' who Jews believe will one day bring a perfect age for everyone that will last forever.
mezuzah	a small box on doorposts of houses and rooms.
midrash	'searching': a story which explains and explores ideas hidden in other stories, especially in the TeNaKh.
Orthodox	keeping the religion according to the halaha (law).
Progressive	Reform or Liberal; interpreting Judaism in the light of modern life.
rabbi	a Jewish religious teacher who may preach and act as a judge. Many rabbis also do community work.
Reform	a form of Judaism which emphasizes the teachings of the TeNaKh more than the Talmud and changes some of the features of Orthodox practice, while keeping the essence of Judaism. See 'Progressive'.
secular	a term for Jewish people who are born Jews and identify with the Jewish people but do not practise the religion.

Sefardi	originating in Spain, and other Mediterranean and Middle Eastern countries. Sefardi Jews spoke Ladino for centuries. This language was similar to medieval Spanish.
Shabbat	the Jewish Sabbath day, which lasts from sunset on Friday until sunset on Saturday.
Shoah	'whirlwind': the Nazi holocaust.
shul	See 'synagogue'.
synagogue	the Jewish place of study, prayer and meeting. Ashkenazi Jews call it 'shul'.
Talmud	'study': a collection of writings, completed in 500 CE, based on rabbis' discussions about right and wrong. It has two parts, the Mishnah and the Gemara.
Temple	the central place of Jewish worship from 1000 BCE to 70 CE, where priests offered sacrifices, in Jerusalem.
TeNaKh	the Jewish Bible, consisting of the Torah, the Nevi'im (prophets) and the Ketuvim (writings).
Torah	the first five books of the Jewish Bible; Jewish teaching (ideas and values); the Jewish way of life.
Yiddish	language spoken by Ashkenazi Jews for centuries, based on medieval German and written in the Hebrew alphabet.
Zionist	believing in the importance of the modern State of Israel, striving to improve the safety and welfare of Israel and to strengthen the society.

Book List

Non–fiction

Chaya Burstein, *The Jewish Kids Catalog*, The Jewish Publication Society of America, 1983 (Facts, stories and lots of activities)

Douglas Charing, *The Jewish World*, Macdonald, 1983

Clive Lawton, *Religion through Festivals: Judaism*, Longman, 1989

Jill Rutter, *Jewish Migrations*, Wayland, 1994

Fiction:

Sholom Aleichem, *Holiday Tales of Sholom Aleichem*, selected and translated by Aliza Shevrin, Macmillan, 1985 (stories on festival themes, set in the Ukrainian Yiddish-speaking Jewish community of old Russia at the end of the nineteenth century)

Lynne Reid Banks, *One More River*, Penguin, 1988 (A Canadian girl goes to live on a kibbutz in Israel just before the Six Day War, and forms a relationship with an Arab boy in a nearby village.)

Judy Blume, *Are you there God? It's me, Margaret*, Pan, 1990 (A teenage girl with one Jewish and one Christian parent talks to God about growing up and her religious and cultural identity.)

Lawrence Bush, *Emma Ansky-Levine and her Mitzvah-Machine*, Union of American Hebrew Congregations Press, 1991 (a fantasy story about a machine that takes her on journeys into the world of Jewish life)

Lois Lowry, *Number the Stars*, HarperCollins, 1991 (A Christian family helps a Jewish family in Denmark in the Second World War.)

Hans Peter Richter, *Friedrich*, translated by Edite Kroll, Penguin, 1970 (A Jewish boy grows up in Germany in the 1930s and 1940s.)

Isaac Bashevis Singer, *When Shlemiel Went to Warsaw and other stories*, translated by the author and Elizabeth Shub, Collins, 1988 (stories set in Eastern Europe)

Fran Weissenberg, *The Streets are Paved with Gold*, Harbinger House, 1990 (a story of growing up as the child of immigrant parents in Brooklyn, New York in 1922)

Note on Dates

Each religion has its own system for counting the years of its history. The starting point may be related to the birth or death of a special person or an important event. In everyday life, today, when different communities have dealings with each other, they need to use the same counting system for setting dates in the future and writing accounts of the past. The Western system is now used throughout the world. It is based on Christian beliefs about Jesus: AD (Anno Domini = in the year of our Lord) and BC (Before Christ). Members of the various world faiths use the common Western system, but, instead of AD and BC, they say and write CE (in the Common Era) and BCE (before the Common Era).

Index